by Louise Nelson

Minneapolis, Minnesota

**Credits**
All images are courtesy of Shutterstock.com, unless otherwise specified. With thanks to Getty Images, Thinkstock Photo, and iStockphoto. Front Cover – Macrovector, benchart, dizzzdergunov, Inspiring. 4–5 – Daiquiri, AboutLife, Motortion Films. 6–7 – Matusciac Alexandru, Feng Yu. 8–9 – IgorZh, Riccardo Piccinini, Oksana Ph, Dreamframer. 10–11 – Marc Ward, Dima Zel, NancyLieder, CC BY-SA 4.0, via Wikimedia Commons, Merlin74, Jurik Peter, SkyPics Studio. 12–13 – Merlin74, Luma creative, True Touch Lifestyle, Allexxandar, Jacob Lund. 14–15 – ktsdesign, CloudOnePhoto, WindVector, Naeblys, Dudeanatortron, CC BY-SA 4.0, via Wikimedia Commons, Alexander_P, Fort Worth Star-Telegram Photograph Collection, Special Collections, The University of Texas at Arlington Library, Arlington, Texas, Art Kovalenco. 16–17 – Eugene Berman, Imagewell, Courtesy, Fort Worth Star-Telegram Photograph Collection, Special Collections, The University of Texas at Arlington Library, Arlington, Texas. 18–19 – Ursatii, medvedsky.kz, Stephen G M, Numstocker, Melkor3D, K.i.f, CC BY-SA 3.0, via Wikimedia Commons, StudioIlanP. 20–21 – Ian Peter Morton, FOTOKITA, Atstock Productions, Limbitech. 22–23 – Nerthuz, Vlad Siaber, ESA/DLR/FU Berlin (G. Neukum), CC BY-SA 3.0 IGO, via Wikimedia Commons, space.com, CC BY-SA 4.0, via Wikimedia Commons. 24–25 – vectortatu, Potemin Anton, LOUIS-MICHEL DESERT, sergio34, Mickes Photos. 26–27 – The original uploader was El C at English Wikipedia. CC BY-SA 2.5, via Wikimedia Commons, ESA; RegoLight, visualisation: Liquifer Systems Group, 2018, CC BY-SA 3.0, via Wikimedia Commons, Event Horizon Telescope, CC BY 4.0, via Wikimedia Commons, Siberian Art, Nawadoln. 28–29 – ANDRIY B, Pablo Carlos Budassi, CC BY-SA 4.0, via Wikimedia Commons, CNSA, CC BY 4.0, via Wikimedia Commons, janez volmajer. 30–31 – PeopleImages.com – Yuri A, Photographielove, Oksana Chistova, Eloku, TheMeteor.

**Bearport Publishing Company Product Development Team**
President: Jen Jenson; Director of Product Development: Spencer Brinker; Managing Editor: Allison Juda; Associate Editor: Naomi Reich; Associate Editor: Tiana Tran; Senior Designer: Colin O'Dea; Associate Designer: Elena Klinkner; Associate Designer: Kayla Eggert; Product Development Specialist: Anita Stasson

Library of Congress Cataloging-in-Publication Data is available at www.loc.gov or upon request from the publisher.

ISBN: 979-8-88822-002-3 (hardcover)
ISBN: 979-8-88822-186-0 (paperback)
ISBN: 979-8-88822-317-8 (ebook)

© 2024 BookLife Publishing
This edition is published by arrangement with BookLife Publishing.

North American adaptations © 2024 Bearport Publishing Company. All rights reserved. No part of this publication may be reproduced in whole or in part, stored in any retrieval system, or transmitted in any form or by any means, electronic, mechanical, photocopying, recording, or otherwise, without written permission from the publisher.

For more information, write to Bearport Publishing, 5357 Penn Avenue South, Minneapolis, MN 55419.

# CONTENTS

Welcome to TNT ..................... 4
The Moon Landing .................. 6
Nibiru ............................. 10
UFOs .............................. 14
Alien Abduction ................... 18
Life on Mars ...................... 22
Totally Out There! ................ 26
Sensible Science .................. 30
Glossary .......................... 31
Index ............................. 32
Read More ......................... 32
Learn More Online ................. 32

# Welcome to TNT

## TOTALLY NOT TRUE

There are many incredible things about space. How can we know what's true? Let's use science to explode totally-not-true stories and leave only facts behind.

Some of the strangest stories about space seem real. We need to **investigate** to try and understand them. Then, we can find out what gets blown apart by science.

Let's use the scientific method. It helps us find **evidence** to learn what we can trust.

# The Scientific Method

The scientific method uses these steps.

| | |
|---|---|
| **Step 1:** Ask a question. | Is my brother an alien? |
| **Step 2:** Make a guess. | Yes. He does very strange things. |
| **Step 3:** Find evidence. | Check how many eyes he has. |
| **Step 4:** Answer your question. | He has only two eyes. Aliens have many. He's not an alien. |
| **Step 5:** Ask a new question and do it again. | Maybe he's just weird. More investigation needed! |

**Warning!** Some evidence in this book may be misleading or have a different explanation. Look out for this stamp.

LET'S GET EXPLODING!

# The Moon Landing

### One Small Step for Man or One Big Lie?

In 1969, Neil Armstrong took the first-ever steps on the moon. Some people thought this was too unbelievable to be true. Let's look at the reasons some people think this moment was really recorded on Earth.

IT'S A TRICK!

LOOKS JUST LIKE THIS FLAG ON EARTH.

### The Flag

Armstrong stuck a flag on the moon. It looked like it was blowing in the wind. But there isn't any wind in space.

### Where Are the Stars?

None of the pictures of the moon landing have stars. Is this because the pictures weren't actually taken in space?

Missing stars?

## Shady Shadows

Shadows in the photos are pointed many ways. Is that because they were made by lights on a film set rather than the sun?

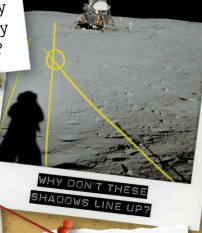

WHY DON'T THESE SHADOWS LINE UP?

Lights in different places would make strange shadows.

## Deadly Radiation

Earth is surrounded by deadly **radiation** from something called the Van Allen radiation belt. Astronauts going to the moon would have to go through it. They wouldn't have survived the trip.

Not dead!

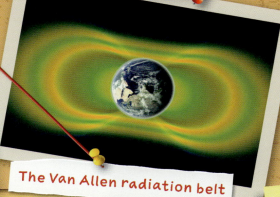

The Van Allen radiation belt

7

# Let's blow it up with science. KABOOM!

THE REAL EVIDENCE!

## The Flag

The moon's flag is held up by a pole across the top. The wrinkles are from how it was folded during the flight. The moon doesn't have enough gravity to straighten it. This creates the **illusion** of wind when there isn't any.

## The Stars

Even though the sky looked dark in the photos, it was actually daytime on the moon. You can't see the stars during the day on Earth because it is too bright. It's the same on the moon.

No stars during daytime!

The camera can't see stars here, either. It's too bright!

LONG SHADOWS MADE BY THE SUN SHOW PERSPECTIVE.

## Shadows

Tilted shadows happen because of something called **perspective**. Objects that aren't next to each other may look odd in shadows.

## Radiation

The astronauts didn't stay in the Van Allen radiation belt long enough to be killed. Their spacecraft traveled so quickly that they only experienced a small amount of radiation.

FLYING THROUGH RADIATION IS SIMILAR TO RUNNING THROUGH RAIN. IF YOU RUN THROUGH RAIN QUICKLY ENOUGH, YOU ONLY GET A LITTLE WET.

EXPLODED BY SCIENCE!

9

# Nibiru

Some people believe there is a giant, undiscovered planet called Nibiru on its way toward Earth. Will it crash into us?

Nibiru?   Earth

CRASHING PLANETS

NANCY LIEDER

## Nancy Lieder and the Aliens

Aliens said so! In 1995, a woman named Nancy Lieder got a message from aliens through a device in her brain. The aliens warned her about Nibiru's arrival.

## But Wait, There's More

The aliens warned Lieder that Nibiru would arrive in 2003. After 2003 passed without Nibiru showing up, Lieder revealed she had been given the wrong date . . . on purpose! The false date was supposed to confuse people on Earth.

AN ALIEN?

10

## The Kuiper Belt

The strong gravity from a planet as large as Nibiru would cause some objects in space to move around. Is this happening? Some people have noticed unusual movements of objects in the Kuiper Belt.

THE KUIPER BELT IS A PART OF OUR SOLAR SYSTEM THAT IS FULL OF SPACE OBJECTS.

## The Sumerians

Ancient **Sumerians** may have seen Nibiru thousands of years ago. The planet must have been close if people were able to see it without **telescopes**.

The Sumerians made images of the planet on stone tablets.

11

# Let's get exploding!

## An Unlikely Story

Lieder never gave any evidence to prove the aliens were real, that she had a device in her brain, or that Nibiru actually exists. A story without evidence to support it is not a good source of information.

## Changing Stories

Lieder's warning about Nibiru still hasn't come true, even though the date has changed many times. When details of a story change again and again, it often means the story isn't true.

## Not What You Think

We would expect unusual movement in space objects closer than the Kuiper Belt if Nibiru was getting closer. It would also affect the planets near Earth. But scientists haven't seen any changes by our planet.

## A Stone-Cold Trail

Most **experts** say that the Sumerian carvings just show made-up stories. This isn't evidence of the planet Nibiru.

EXPLODED BY SCIENCE!

# UFOs

An unidentified flying object is often called a UFO. Some people think UFOs are really alien spacecraft.

Could UFOs look like the ones in this image?

## UFOs in Area 51

Area 51 is a top-secret Air Force base in the Nevada desert, but it may not be secret enough. Many people say they have seen mysterious UFOs flying around Area 51. Could these be alien ships?

NO ONE IS ALLOWED PAST HERE.

## Suspiciously Secret

The U.S. government keeps a lot of information hidden. There was once a secret team whose job was to learn about UFOs. Government officials must know more than they're telling us!

WHAT ARE THEY HIDING?

## Bob Lazar

BOB LAZAR

We might have secret information from inside Area 51. Bob Lazar said that when he worked in Area 51, he saw an alien spacecraft. He said he even helped the government build a new version of the ship.

THE UFO LAZAR SAW LOOKED A LOT LIKE THIS.

## The Roswell Incident

In 1947, bits of a crashed UFO were found in Roswell, New Mexico. The parts didn't look like they were from a normal aircraft. The government quickly swooped in to hide the evidence.

Newspapers called this a flying saucer.

BITS FROM AN ALIEN UFO?

15

# TIME FOR TNT!

### Identified!

Area 51 was a testing site for secret airplanes. These spy planes flew much higher than other planes, which is why people couldn't tell what they were.

### I Spy

The government's UFO team was not looking for alien spacecraft. Instead, they were looking for secret airplanes from other countries. The government didn't want other countries to know about their spy planes, but they did want to know about any planes spying on them!

WHO IS BOB LAZAR?

## Bob Who?

Lazar told an interesting story, but no one could back it up. In fact, there weren't even records to show that Lazar ever worked at Area 51.

## Project Mogul

The Roswell UFO was part of a top-secret plan called Project Mogul. Big balloons carried microphones into the sky to listen for bombs. The crashed balloon looked alien to some people because it was from new technology made specially for Project Mogul—not for an alien spacecraft!

Keeping records helps us check if something really happened and if a story is trustworthy.

A Project Mogul balloon probably looked similar to this.

EXPLODED BY SCIENCE!

# Alien Abduction

Betty and Barney Hill were some of the first people to claim they'd been **abducted** by aliens. At first, they didn't fully remember what happened. But later, the Hills did remember aliens running medical tests on them inside a UFO.

THE HILLS REMEMBERED A BRIGHT UFO.

## Suspicious Scuffs

The couple had marks and scuffs on their clothes from the time when they lost their memories. Betty had a torn dress and Barney had marks on top of one shoe.

Was Barney dragged across the ground by aliens?

## Matching Stories

A doctor helped the Hills get their memories back. Lots of what Betty and Barney remembered was the same.

BETTY REMEMBERED AN ALIEN POKING HER WITH A NEEDLE!

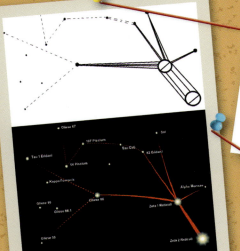

Both remembered lying on a table while gray aliens stood around them.

MATCHING STORIES ARE OFTEN A SIGN THAT SOMETHING COULD BE TRUE.

## Star Map

Betty also remembered a star map an alien had shown her. Her drawing of the map looked very similar to a group of stars called Zeta Reticuli.

Matching maps!

# Let's explode that misleading evidence!

## Meaningless Marks

The marks the Hills noticed on their clothes could have come from all sorts of things. The scrapes on Barney's shoe and the tear in Betty's dress could have happened by just catching on a rock or branch.

There are lots of ways their clothes could have been damaged. This evidence isn't strong enough to support an alien abduction.

Were the marks already there before they lost their memories?

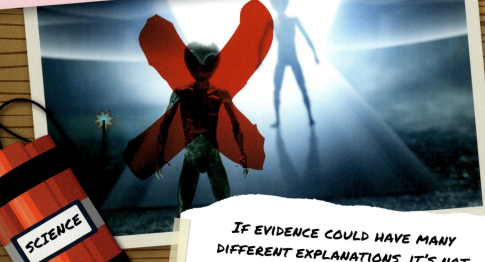

If evidence could have many different explanations, it's not strong evidence. Strong evidence usually points to only one answer.

## Just a Dream?

Sometimes, people can create false memories of things that didn't happen. This can occur when people are asked questions in a certain way. Even the Hills's doctor thought the memories came from a dream and not real life!

## Not a Match

Betty's star map doesn't match Zeta Reticuli as closely as people first believed. Scientists now have better ways to map stars. The newer maps of Zeta Reticuli aren't like Betty's drawing.

Plus, there aren't any planets near Zeta Reticuli.

**EXPLODED BY SCIENCE!**

21

# Life on Mars

Are there other planets in our solar system with creatures who look like us? Let's find out why some people believe Martians are real.

## Face the Truth

This picture from Mars shows something surprisingly familiar. The giant face could have been made by a **civilization** of Martians!

Can you see the eye, nose, and lips?

## Pyramids

These pyramids on Mars don't look natural. Could they have been built by a Martian civilization? They look similar to the pyramids the Egyptians built on Earth long ago.

MARS: MARTIAN MADE?

EARTH: HUMAN MADE

## Alien Art

The ground on Mars is covered with things that look like huge drawings. One photo from Mars shows the shape of an elephant head. Another photo shows a giant smiley face.

*Making shapes this big would take lots of Martians working together.*

ELEPHANT

SMILEY FACE

## Trees

Art isn't the only thing that's been spotted on Mars. Some images show what appear to be trees.

23

# TIME TO BLOW UP SOME FALSE IDEAS!

## The Face on Mars

From a different direction the face looks like a normal hill. Shadows just made it look like a face.

Nothing alien about this!

New photos were taken with better cameras. The dark spots that looked like nostrils aren't there.

No nose

## All-Natural

Pyramid shapes in nature aren't as unusual as people might think. There are many pyramid-shaped mountains on Earth that haven't been made by people.

On Earth, the Matterhorn is a mountain even more pyramid-shaped than those on Mars.

24

## Can You Believe Your Eyes?

Scientists have proven that our eyes can play tricks on us. We may see something familiar in random shapes. The elephant was actually made from a **lava flow** across the surface of Mars, not aliens.

CAN YOU SEE THE SHAPE OF A PERSON IN THESE CLOUDS?

### Sand

The tree shapes in the photos of Mars are most likely from dark sand. The patterns are made when heat from the sun causes a gas under the surface to burst. This pushes dark sand out from under the red dust.

EXPLODED BY SCIENCE!

25

# Totally Out There!

## The Boötes Void

Most of our night sky is filled with stars and **galaxies**. However, a huge area called the Boötes Void is missing thousands of galaxies. Could aliens have caused this by hiding all the stars around them?

THE VOID HAS FEW TO NO GALAXIES.

## Secret Moon Base?

Because of the way the moon spins, we always see the same side of it from Earth. Does the side we can't see hide a secret moon base?

The secret base might look like this.

## Black Holes

Black holes are **invisible** things in space that make everything near them disappear. How do we know they exist if we can't see them?

Where is the light going?

## It's All about Earth

The sun passes over our heads every day. Does this mean the sun is going around Earth? Is Earth at the center of the solar system?

The sun definitely looks like it is moving down.

# LET'S TNT EVERYTHING THAT'S NOT TRUE!

## The Boötes Void

The Boötes Void isn't a single large empty area but several smaller areas grouped together. This is not uncommon. It's not so alien after all!

Grouped-up voids act a bit like grouped-up bubbles of empty space.

## Nothing to See Here

We can't see the far side of the moon from Earth, but we have seen it from space. Astronauts that have **orbited** the moon haven't seen anything unusual there.

## Black Holes

Black holes really exist! They have very strong gravity that pulls in everything around them, including light. We can't see black holes, but we can see how they affect other things in space.

BLACK HOLES ARE IN THE CENTERS OF GALAXIES

## In a Spin

As Earth orbits the sun, it rotates, too. Each full rotation is 24 hours. During the day, we see the sun because we're on the side of Earth that's turned toward it. At night, our side of Earth is turned away from the sun.

**EXPLODED BY SCIENCE!**

29

# Sensible Science

Aliens building things on Mars may seem cool, even if it isn't real. And something as unbelievable as a black hole is real.

When we aren't sure what to believe, gathering evidence and using the scientific method can help us explode stories that aren't true.

Next time you hear about something that doesn't have much scientific evidence, don't just believe it! Put your science skills to the test. *Kaboom!*

# GLOSSARY

**abducted** taken away against one's will

**civilization** a large group of people, or possibly aliens, that share the same history and way of life

**evidence** objects or information that can be used to prove whether something is true

**experts** people who know a lot about a subject

**galaxies** collections of billions of stars and other space objects held together by gravity

**illusion** a misleading image that tricks the mind

**investigate** to search for information about something

**invisible** unable to be seen

**lava flow** a stream of hot liquid rock

**orbited** moved in a path around another object

**perspective** the appearance of objects with respect to their distance and positions in relation to each other

**radiation** a type of energy that can be very dangerous

**Sumerians** people who lived about 6,000 years ago in a place that was where Iraq is today

**telescopes** tools that use lenses and mirrors to make distant objects appear larger

# INDEX

airplanes 16
Area 51 14–17
black holes 27, 29–30
face 22–24
flag 6, 8
governments 14–16
gravity 8, 11, 29
Kuiper Belt 11, 13
Lazar, Bob 15, 17
Lieder, Nancy 10, 12
Mars 22–25, 30
moon 6–8, 26, 28
Nibiru 10–13
planets 10–11, 13, 22
Project Mogul 17
radiation 7, 9
solar systems 11, 22, 27
stars 6, 8, 19, 21, 26
stone 11, 13
sun 7, 9, 25, 27, 29
UFOs 14–19
Zeta Reticuli 19, 21

# READ MORE

**Gleisner, Jenna Lee.** *UFOs (In Search of the Unexplained).* Minneapolis: Kaleidoscope, 2021.

**Hoena, Blake.** *The Roswell UFO Incident (Paranormal Mysteries).* Minneapolis: Bellwether Media, 2020.

**Hustad, Douglas.** *Fact and Fiction of the Space Age (Fact and Fiction of American History).* Minneapolis: Abdo Publishing, 2022.

# LEARN MORE ONLINE

1. Go to **www.factsurfer.com** or scan the QR code below.
2. Enter "**Not True Space**" into the search box.
3. Click on the cover of this book to see a list of websites.